Ann Ayre Hely
A Crimean War Nurse
from Ravenstone, Leicestershire

Other books by Wendy Freer:

Women and Children of the Cut (RCHS 1995)

Canal Boatmen's Missions (with Gill Foster, RCHS 2004)

Ashby de la Zouch and the Ashby Poor Law Union
(Ashby Museum, 2012)

All of a Lather, Soap Manufacture in Ashby de la Zouch 1890-2011
(with Alvyn Owen and Derick Owen, Ashby Museum, 2013)

Doing Their Bit, Ashby Girls' Wartime Harvest Camps, 1942-1944, (Pudding Bag Productions, 2015)

Ann Ayre Hely
A Crimean War Nurse
from Ravenstone, Leicestershire

by Wendy Freer

Pudding Bag Productions
2016

Copyright © 2016 by Wendy Freer

All rights reserved. This book, or any portion thereof, may not be reproduced or used in any manner whatsoever without the express written permission of the publisher except for the use of brief quotations in a book review or scholarly journal.

First Printing: 2016

ISBN 978-1-326-88840-4

Pudding Bag Productions
68 Wood Street, Ashby de la Zouch,
Leicestershire, LE65 1EG

wendyfreer.org.uk

Contents

Acknowledgements	**v**
Portrait of Ann Ayre Hely	**vi**
1. Early Life	**1**
2. The Crimean War and the Care of the Sick and Wounded	**4**
3. The Setting up of Smyrna Hospital	**8**
4. Ann Hely Answers the Call	**10**
5. Nursing in Smyrna Hospital	**13**
6. Transfer to Renkioi Hospital	**24**
7. The Building of Renkioi Hospital	**25**
8. The Staffing and Organisation of Renkioi Hospital	**31**
9. The Work of Renkioi Hospital	**35**
10. Bashi Bazooks	**39**
11. Later life	**42**
Appendix 1 Staff of Renkioi Hospital	**47**
Appendix 2 *Leicester Chronicle* report 18th Dec 1897	**50**
References	**55**
Short Bibliography	**57**
Index	**58**

Acknowledgements

The author would like to thank Ravenstone Hospital Trust for their support of this project and for allowing access to material in their archive. Special thanks are due to Adrian Argyle, clerk to the Trustees, Ann Thorne, Trustee and Mary Danaher, former Chair of the Trust.

Thanks are also due to the National Archives for permission to reproduce the photograph of Ann Ayre Hely on page vi.

The publication of this book has been partly funded with a Shire Grant from Leicestershire County Council Museum Support Service.

Ann Ayre Hely. She is seen here wearing the Order of the Royal Red Cross, presented to her in December 1897.
In the background can be seen Ravenstone Hospital.
Reproduced by permission of the National Archives.

1 Early Life

Ann Ayre (Eyre) Hely was born Ann Ayre Bradshaw, in the Leicestershire village of Ravenstone on 7th November 1819. She was a seemingly ordinary village woman from an unremarkable family, yet she went on to lead an extraordinary life and to receive national recognition for her work in the Crimean War.

We know very little of her early life. Her father was John Bradshaw, born in the village in 1787. He married Sarah Saddler in 1804 and worked as a blacksmith. He also rented a public house in the village, *The Plough Inn,* and three acres of glebe land on Church Lane, from Lord Fosbrooke.[1] When he died in 1838, his wife continued as the publican of *The Plough.* She is shown as innkeeper in the 1851 Census along with Ann, and Ann's 20-year old brother Henry. They are described as innkeeper's daughter and innkeeper's son, so presumably they were working with their mother in the inn.[2] Ann had several siblings. In 1851, her 28-year-old brother, William, was also living at home. His occupation was given as blacksmith. Next door, her 27-year-old brother, Thomas, was living with his wife and three children. He too worked as a blacksmith and the family was able to afford a live-in 14-year-old general servant girl.

Ann's future husband, John Joseph Hely, had come to live and work in the village some time between 1841 and 1846. He was an Irishman who, according to the 1841 Census, was a member of the Royal College of Surgeons, Edinburgh, which is presumably where he trained.[3] At the time of the 1841 Census, he had been living in Marylebone, London, where he was working as an assistant surgeon.[4]

By 1846, he had been living in Ravenstone long enough to have earned a good reputation with some at least. Some of the women who were living in Ravenstone Hospital almshouses at that time were in the habit of sending for him when they were in need of medical attention. This did not meet with the approval of the Hospital authorities, who employed several resident nurses to look after the women, and retained the services of a doctor in Ashby de la Zouch. The Master of the Hospital, the Reverend Webb, *"gave orders to the nurses not to come for [Dr. Hely] when these females should require [his] attendance."* This, in turn, upset Dr. Hely, who wrote to the trustees on 7th September 1846 protesting that:

"these orders contain an act of injustice to me and to these females who choose to employ me and in my own defence, and in compliance with their wishes, I have taken the liberty of laying the case before you in order to ascertain whether or not they are to be deprived of the attendance of the nurses on account of having me for their medical attendant."[5]

Whether or not the trustees took note of Dr. Hely's complaint is not recorded.

We do not know how Ann met and got to know John Hely, but according to a report in the *Leicester Chronicle* on 12th August 1854, the doctor *"had been of intemperate habits, and drank ardent spirits to great excess."* It may then be supposed that he frequented *The Plough Inn* and that they became acquainted there.

Whatever the circumstances of their courtship, they were married in August 1851. Their marriage was short, childless, and came to an end with the unfortunate death of John Hely in August 1854. Both the *Leicester Chronicle* and the *Leicester Journal* reported on the coroner's inquest, which took place in *The Plough Inn* on Saturday 5th August. There it was said that Dr. Hely had got up in the night and accidently drank a tumbler of wine of colchicum, thinking it to be sherry. It appeared that the original bottle containing this liquid had been broken the previous day and consequently it had been poured into another bottle, which was labeled "Sweet spirits of nitre". Small doses of wine of colchicum were used for the treatment of gout, gouty rheumatism and neuralgia, but in large quantities it is a fatal poison. Having swallowed a whole glassful, Dr. Hely was immediately seized with a bout of violent sickness. He was seen by Mr. Paterson, the Ibstock surgeon, and later by Mr. Wood of Shepshed, but the pain in his bowels increased, and he died soon after midnight the following day. Despite the fact that he was a Roman Catholic, his remains were interred in Ravenstone churchyard the following Sunday.[6]

What became of Ann Hely immediately following the death of her husband is not recorded, but she appears to have been a very capable and resourceful woman who did not wait long before seeking to make herself useful to others.

2 The Crimean War and the care of the sick and wounded

The causes of this war are complex, but may be put in simple terms as a combination of religious differences and competition for influence in the region, particularly with Turkey.

The area was strategically important for Britain and France, who were anxious to protect their trade routes to the East, and worried about Russian expansion. Religious tensions between Catholic France and Orthodox Russia over control of the religious sites, came to a head in 1853, when riots in Bethlehem led to the killing of a number of Orthodox monks. As the town was part of the Ottoman Empire, Russia made a number of demands on Turkey with the aim of resolving the issues in favour of the Orthodox Church. These demands were not met, and Russia mobilized her army against Turkey in July 1853. Turkey responded by declaring war on Russia in October of the same year.

Britain and France declared war on Russia in March 1854 and mustered their forces at Varna in Bulgaria. Their plan was to launch an all-out attack on Russian forces in the Crimea and seize Sevastopol. Given their naval supremacy, the British did not expect the conflict to last long, but they were to be proved wrong.

It was not until September of 1854 that a joint invasion force of British, French and Turkish troops landed at Kalamatia Bay, north of Sevastopol. Their move south led to the first set-piece battle of the war, which took place at Alma. The Russians were forced back, and there were heavy casualties on both sides, although the Russians suffered far more.

The allied forces moved on to besiege Sevastopol, but were unable to cut off Russian supplies to the north of the city. On 25th October, the Russians began to advance towards the British lines, and this resulted in the Battle of Balaklava and the infamous "Charge of the Light Brigade". This latter was a fiasco, and only a charge by the

French cavalry saved the Light Brigade from total destruction. The battle ended with the Russians retaining their guns and their position, although they had failed to break through British lines. Casualties were extremely heavy on both sides.

Even before this disastrous battle, news had begun to filter back to the public in Britain about the horrors of the war, the appalling casualty rate, and the dreadful conditions in such hospitals and medical centres as existed. In September 1854, *The Times* war correspondent, William H Russell, had brought the desperate conditions in the Crimea to the attention of the British public and popularised the call for women nurses to join the forces, writing:

"Are there no devoted women amongst us, able and willing to go forth to minister to the sick and suffering soldiers of the East in the hospitals of Scutari? Are none of the daughters of England, at this extreme hour of need, ready for such a work of mercy?"[7]

Lady Maria Forrester, the daughter of Lord Roden, contacted Sydney Herbert, who was then Secretary at War responsible for the War Office, offering to organize a scheme for sending nurses to the Crimea. Herbert doubted her ability to do so, however, and felt that the nurses she had in mind probably had no idea of the horrors and difficulties that they would be facing.[8] On the 15th October, he wrote to Florence Nightingale, asking her to consider taking charge of nursing operations in Scutari, Turkey.

Nightingale agreed, and on the evening of Saturday, 20th October 1854, she departed for Paris, followed two days later by thirty-eight or forty[9] nurses:

"some of them highly educated and accomplished, some experienced in their calling, but all devoted to their work of charity."

They were to set sail on the 26th October for Constantinople on the *Vectis*.

Nightingale and her team of nurses arrived in Scutari, Turkey in early November 1854 and were confronted with appalling conditions in the hospital there.

In 1854, there was no system for calling up civilian medical practitioners in an emergency, although volunteers could put themselves forward. Some civilian doctors had been attached to the hospital at Scutari since October 1854; others were working there unofficially. Some medical students also went out to work as dressers.

Reports in the press on the shortage of medical staff in the war zone were putting pressure on the authorities to bring in civilian staff. On 29th January 1855, the Duke of Newcastle stated in the House of Lords:

"In the present state of the Army and of the hospitals, it will be absolutely necessary, in spite of all opposition and all profound feelings to the contrary, to introduce into the Army Hospitals the civilian element."[10]

It is well known that popular opinion at this time was against the idea that female nurses could be of any use in the Crimea. It was not only the women, however, who were unwanted by the military. The proposal to set up civil hospitals, staffed entirely by civilian doctors, greatly upset the army medical staff. Resentment was caused by the fact that civilian staff were better paid, and it was also felt that the plan suggested the army doctors were poorly trained and not capable of looking after the sick and wounded themselves.

Dirty, overcrowded hospitals, rampant disease, as well as terrible wounds, an appallingly high death rate and an overworked, under resourced staff of military personnel, filled with resentment towards civilian doctors and nurses – these were the obstacles faced by Florence Nightingale and her nurses on their arrival. They lost no time in setting out to overcome them and were to be followed over the next three or four months by other civilians, amongst them, Mrs. Ann Ayre Hely.

3 The Setting up of Smyrna Hospital

The winter of 1854-55 was particularly severe, and the army hospitals in the Crimea and at Scutari were overflowing with men suffering from disease, cold and hunger. Early in the year of 1855, the Turkish barracks at Smyrna were adapted for use as a civil hospital, which was initially intended for convalescent patients.

Patients began to arrive at Smyrna between February and March; 993 arrived during this period. Conditions were grossly overcrowded, and of this first contingent, 127 died. The staff was to consist of a Medical Superintendent, three physicians, five surgeons, six assistant physicians, ten assistant surgeons, and a resident medical officer. There was also to be a secretary, nine dispensers, a civil engineer, and only one military officer.[11]

The first of the medical staff to arrive was the surgeon, Thomas Spencer Wells, on 1st March 1855. All the others reached Smyrna by the end of the month. Amongst them was a surgeon named Holmes Coote and his wife. She was appointed Superintendent of Nurses, or Matron.

On their arrival at Smyrna, the female nurses who had accompanied Holmes Coote quickly changed the assumptions of the senior medical staff:

"The few days these ladies had done their duty had been quite sufficient to convince those who had previously entertained doubts as to the utility of such an order of nurses, of the very great assistance they can and will render. Their extreme kindness and patient attention to the sick – the ready comprehension of directions – the perfect manner in which they were enabled to keep these directions in mind by the use of notebooks – the confidence with which they could be entrusted with wines and spirits .... their excellent cookery of sago, arrowroot, light puddings, and various drinks, have established beyond all question, that if they only

continue as they have begun, this experiment in the establishment of hospital sisterhoods must prove a successful one.[12]

In addition to nursing nuns, who went out to some of the hospitals, there were two "classes" of nurses: so-called "lady nurses", who were volunteers (although some were paid) from upper class backgrounds, and "professional nurses", who were paid. Dr. John Meyer, the Medical Superintendent at Smyrna, was later to report that the *"professional nurses worked uncommonly well"*. He was less complimentary about the "lady nurses", many of whom were:

"unfit, from one reason or another, and several were sent home, and after that those that remained did very well indeed ... few are experienced, but they are intelligent and will carry out the orders given."

Spencer Wells, in his introductory address, given on 11th April 1855, also praised the other nurses saying:

"I entertained very considerable misgivings as to the propriety or probable success of this experiment. But a very few days served to dispel all forebodings of evil, and to raise my most sanguine hopes of good."

He said that he found the system of putting *"ladies of education"* in charge of female trained nurses was very successful, and he hoped that the example would be followed in hospitals in England.

4. Ann Hely Answers the Call

One of the nurses, of whom Spencer Wells and other senior medical officers spoke, was Mrs. Ann Ayre Hely.

It is not known how Ann got to hear of the need for nurses. The newspapers, both local and national, had been carrying reports on the crisis throughout 1854, so it is reasonable to assume that she would have been aware of the situation.

Although there is no documentary evidence recording how Ann travelled out, or when exactly she arrived, several pieces of evidence have come to light which allow us to make a reliable assumption.

The Florence Nightingale Museum at St Thomas's Hospital, London, holds a register of nurses sent out "to the East" during the Crimean war. Ann Hely is recorded in it as having been transferred from Smyrna Hospital to Renkioi on November 19th 1855. This is a transcript of the entry:

Name, Country and condition	Age	Residence	Where trained or practised	Guarantee and character	When and where sent	Remarks
Mrs. Hely, Nurse, 18/- a week. Given 2/- a week extra afterwards by the War Office from 1st Nov 1855 to 17 Sept 1856				Good	As above, Renkioi, 19th Dec 1855	18/- a week. Left on Smyrna Hospital breaking up and sent to Renkioi. A very superior woman, a clever nurse, excellent temper, honest, sober, trustworthy & obliging. A great peace-maker amongst others (see report made by Miss Parkes.)

When Ann was awarded the Royal Red Cross in 1897, the event was covered in numerous newspapers across the country. A report in *The Leicester Chronicle,* on 18th December 1897, states that she travelled out to the Crimea with Dr. Holmes Coote and his wife in 1854. As has already been mentioned in the previous chapter, Dr. and Mrs. Coote travelled directly from the UK to Smyrna in March 1855, and it seems highly likely, therefore, that the newspapers got the year wrong, and that Ann arrived in Smyrna in March too. The newspaper report also makes at least two more statements which appear to be inaccurate. Firstly, that she worked in Renkioi from August 1855 until the end of the war. The register of nurses referred to above shows that she was sent to Renkioi in November 1855. Secondly, that the patients at Renkioi were suffering mainly from frostbite and gunshot wounds. Other more reliable sources make it clear that the vast majority of patients in Smyrna and Renkioi hospitals were suffering from diseases such as typhus, dysentery, and other unspecified fevers,[13] although there were quite a number of frostbite cases during the winter months. Perhaps Ann's memory was starting to fail at the time when she was interviewed in 1897 – she would have been 78 years of age – or could it be that some newspaper reporters have always been careless about getting their facts right!

Another very interesting contemporary source adds weight to the theory that Ann travelled to Smyrna in March 1855, and also gives us a wealth of information about what life in the Smyrna hospital would have been like for her.[14] It is a memoir, written anonymously by one of the "lady nurses" who travelled out to Smyrna in March 1855. She does not mention having travelled out with Dr. Coote, but she does say that on their arrival in Smyrna, the Lady Superintendent and her husband were found accommodation in a hotel. That Lady Superintendent, as we learn later on in the book and elsewhere[15], was in fact Mrs. Holmes Coote. The author, who has been identified as being a Martha C Nicol, does mention Mrs. Hely several times, and although she doesn't say very much about Ann herself, she gives us a very clear picture of everyday life for the nurses of Smyrna Hospital. I have drawn on this source extensively in the next chapter.

The paddle steamer "Sinai" which took Lady Nurse Nicol from Marseilles to Malta. Ann Hely would also have been on that voyage. Source: http://www.messageries-maritimes.org/sinai-a.jpg , accessed 11.9.2016

5. Nursing in Smyrna Hospital

For information about Ann's life in Smyrna, I have relied on the anonymously published memoirs of Martha C Nicol, a "lady nurse", who travelled to Smyrna from England in March 1855 and remained there until the hospital closed at the end of the year. Ann Hely was almost certainly on the same ship with her. Although, unlike Ann, she was a "lady nurse", rather than a "professional nurse", her writing tells us much about what life in Smyrna would have been like for Ann.

Martha Nicol and her party set out from London Bridge station for Folkestone on the 3rd March, 1855, at 6 p.m. It was a stormy crossing to Boulogne, which she did not enjoy. They travelled to Paris the following day, and had the opportunity of doing some sightseeing before arriving in Lyon on the night of the 5th March. From there, they sailed down the Rhone to Valence and then travelled to Marseilles by train where they spent at least one night before embarking on the paddle steamer *Sinai* of the *Messagerie Imperiale* shipping line on Thursday, 8th March. They arrived in Malta on Sunday, 11th March, *"in the midst of wind and rain"* where it was too rough for the ship to get into the regular harbour. They arrived at Smyrna on the morning of Thursday, 15th March.

They had rather a miserable and disappointing reception when their ship docked in heavy rain, as no accommodation had been arranged for them, and the only two hotels in the town were full. Eventually, accommodation for Ann and the other nurses was found in the Hotel D'Orient. Dr. and Mrs. Coote went to the other (unnamed) hotel, and the Lady Nurses (all sixteen of them!) were billeted with various members of the Zipcy family; this was the family of the wife of a M. Guidici who *"purveyed for the hospital"*.

The nurses were found accommodation in the hospital the day after their arrival and presumably started work straight a way.

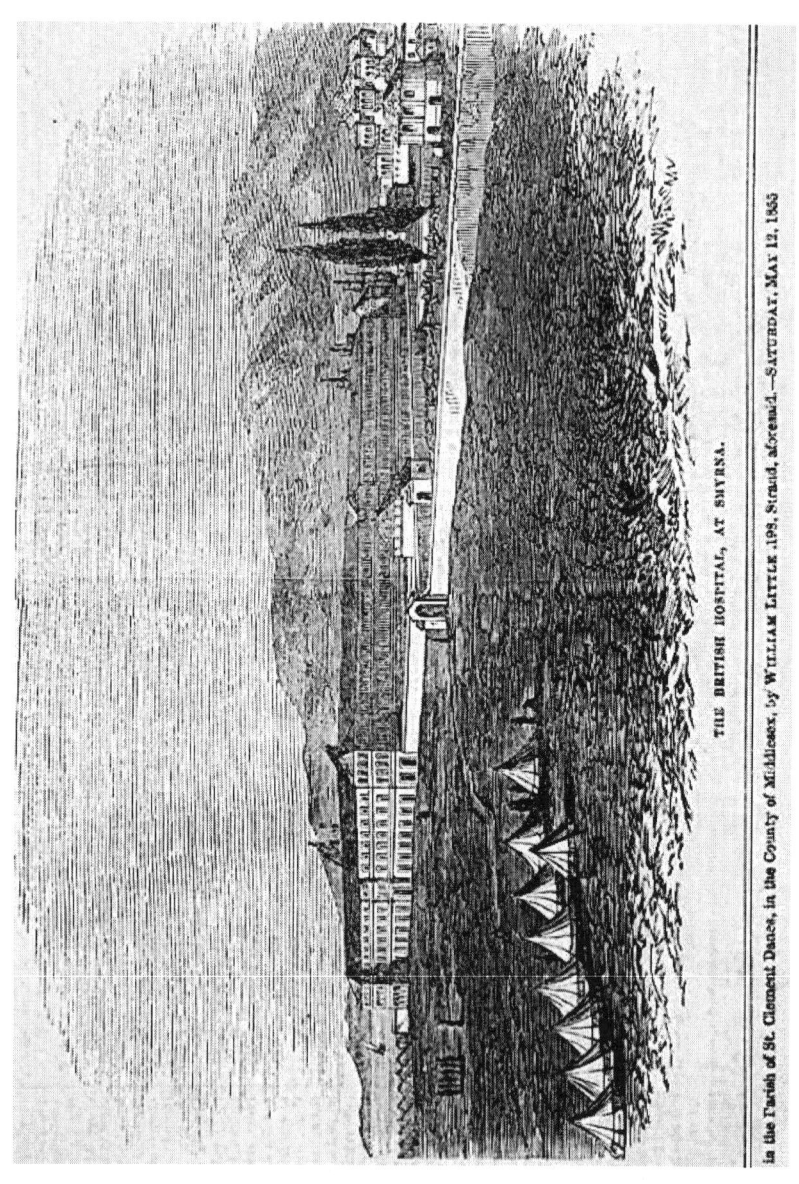

Smyrna Hospital. Source: London Illustrated News, 12th May 1855.

The "lady nurses" did not start work until after a house was found for them to live in, which did not happen until the following Monday, 19th March. They began work on 20th March 1855.

There were between 800 and 1,000 patients in the hospital when the nurses arrived, and there had been a high death rate amongst them. There were a large number of frostbite cases, and many of them were quite horrific. Several men had lost half their feet, and Lady Nurse Nicol describes the case of one young man whose feet were in such a state that *"great pieces of toe came off with the dressing every morning, leaving the bones quite bare."* Many of the men were in such a wretched state when they were brought in that their clothes had to be cut off them outside and burnt. Many were suffering from chest complaints brought on by *"exposure to the cold, or by hurts and blows in the trenches"* and there were about ten deaths a day from *"the worst kind of spotted typhus."*

John Shepherd, in his book on the British Medical Services in the Crimean War, gives the following figures for admissions and deaths:[16]

	Admissions	Deaths
Fevers	416	38
Bowel diseases	345	67
Frostbite	162	18
Scurvy	137	14
Rheumatic diseases	107	4
Wounded	32	0

The hospital was divided into sections referred to as "divisions". We are not told by Lady Nurse Nicol how many wards were in the Smyrna divisions. It was evidently more than one as she says at one point that part of her division was in the basement and another part was on an upper floor – which obviously necessitated a lot of running up and down stairs. The basement was said to be rough and draughty because the long corridor linking the wards had no doors at either end. This made it very uncomfortable in winter, but the cool breeze was welcome in the hot summer months.

The ratio of patients to nurses was high. When she first started, Lady Nurse Nicol had just one nurse with her to look after sixty to eighty patients, although there were also a number of male orderlies. Later she describes the organization of the hospital as follows:

"At first the hospital had eight divisions, with three physicians or surgeons each, two ladies, two nurses, one ward-master and one orderly to every ten or twelve beds in each – there were latterly only four divisions, three physicians or surgeons, one lady, three nurses, one ward-master, and the same number of orderlies as before."

The conditions of work, as well as the living arrangements, were quite different for the lady nurses and the nurses. Lady nurses started work at 9 a.m. and finished at 5 or 6 p.m. They were not expected to work nights, although apparently, many of them did volunteer to do so. The nurses started work at 6 a.m. and were on duty until 8.30 p.m. One of the lady nurses was designated the "Chief Sister of the Division", and she was on duty from 8 a.m. until 5 p.m. The second lady nurse, where there was one, was designated Second Sister and could deputise for the Chief Sister if she was absent.

Lady Nurse Nicol gives a detailed description of the duties and responsibilities of each class of nursing staff. These can be summarised as follows:

Lady nurses and nurses throughout the establishment, acted under the orders of the Medical Superintendent (Dr. Meyer), communicated by the Lady Superintendent (Mrs. Coote).

Chief Sister of Division
She had immediate charge of wards and corridors in the division and sisters, nurses, ward-master and male attendants attached. She was responsible for bedding, linen, dressings and utensils. She was to visit each ward frequently to see that regulations and orders were strictly adhered to. She was to see that meals were served at the right times and that the correct allowances were given, including "extras" such as wine and special foods. She was to enforce strict cleanliness

in the wards and see that bedding etc. was changed whenever necessary. She saw that bed-head tickets were accurate and up-to-date.

Second Sister
She assisted the Chief Sister and deputised for her. She would take a portion of the patients to administer drinks and medicine to them.

Nurses
They were under the superintendence of the Chief Sisters of their division and carried out the orders of the Medical Officer. They dressed wounds and cared for patients in any way directed. They administered, as directed, wine, medicine, and drinks and reported any sudden changes in a patient to the Chief Sister or Medical Officer. They were to take night duty when called upon to do so.

Ward-masters and orderlies
Ward-masters were in charge of the orderlies, but worked under the supervision of the Lady Nurses or Sisters. They had charge of linen and food stuffs, but were directed by the senior nurse.

Food allowances
Poultry was cheap and plentiful, but beef and mutton could be of poor quality, especially the beef. The men were given an allowance of fresh meat each day, but they often complained that they were not given enough.

Fish was available only at irregular intervals because the Greek fishermen did not go to sea regularly.

Potatoes were scarcely grown locally, and the hospital obtained only a poor supply from Malta. There was an ample supply of locally grown fruit and vegetables, which were also very cheap, but despite that, the only vegetables served to the patients usually were potatoes from Malta and "a little green stuff" which was put into the soup. Fruit was only allowed on medical grounds. Lady Nurse Nicol expressed her dismay at this, as there was *"much scurvy and scorbutic affection among the men.*" The bread was of good quality, and there was plenty of rice and barley.

Milk was very difficult to obtain, as cows were kept mainly for beef and not as dairy cattle. Goats' milk was available and was sometimes mixed with asses' milk, but in summer this kept fresh for less than an hour, even when heated over the fire immediately after milking. This was a great inconvenience, as milk was much called for in the patients' diets.

"Extras," which could be ordered by the doctors included:
beef tea, veal broth, chicken broth;
extra bread;
sago, arrowroot, rice, milk;
puddings made of sago, rice, bread, sugar, milk, eggs, ginger or cinnamon;
extra meat;
port wines, Marsala, Hollands (wine), brandy, porter and country wines;
apples, oranges, lemons and other fruits in season, but only as a means of treating disease;
lemonade, orangeade, barley water and gruel.

Sometimes, it was difficult to get the patients to eat, and the nurses had to think of different ways of preparing the ingredients to tempt their poor appetites. For example, egg and milk made into a simple egg custard with the addition of a little nutmeg or lemon for flavouring, would sometimes be more appealing to a man who could not face the normal ration.

The superior ranking of the "lady nurses" was resented by some of the nurses. It seems that they had been told before going out to Smyrna that they would be of equal status to the "lady nurses", and when they arrived, and found this not to be the case, they were very much upset by it. They began to attack the "lady nurses" verbally and then turned on each other telling "*such horrible stories .... often found, on investigation, not to be true.*" However, not all the nurses behaved like this. "*Some of them were sensible women, who worked well and strengthened our hands in every way they could."* It seems reasonable to assume that Ann Hely was one of the sensible women, given the brief report made of her in the register of nurses sent to the East:

"A very superior woman, a clever nurse, excellent temper, honest, sober, trustworthy and obliging, a great peace maker amongst others."

Further resentment was caused amongst some of the nurses when they were asked to act as domestic servants to the "lady nurses". Some local people were recruited to look after the "lady nurses" in their houses, but from time to time, nurses were asked to act as cooks or housekeepers. Some of them refused to do this. Others seemed happy to oblige.

The nurses and "lady nurses" all wore the same, or very similar regulation dress, which Lady Nurse Nicol claimed *"made it often unpleasant for us outside."* The local people could not distinguish between the two ranks and, presumably, treated them all in the same way. This caused trouble for the "lady nurses" because *"Many of the nurses, on their days for going out, used to walk into Smyrna and behave in an unbecoming manner."* As a result, Dr. Meyer, the Medical Superintendent, prohibited the nurses from going out except under the care of the Matron. In order to make a further distinction, the "lady nurses" stopped wearing the sashes embroidered with the words *Smyrna Hospital*, while the nurses continued to do so. All the nurses wore grey or lilac dresses, both in the hospital and also when in Smyrna. The "lady nurses" also wore "leghorn hats" in summer which were wide-brimmed straw hats, very good for keeping the sun off the face when temperatures rose to 98 or 100 degrees Fahrenheit in the shade.

With disease rife, there was often much sickness among the staff as well as the patients. Not long after arrival, Ann Hely was one of six nurses taken ill with typhus fever. This particular affliction was

Regulation dress for nurses at Smyrna Hospital. Source: Nicol.

known as the "twenty one day fever", and one curious feature was a terrible sort of loud screaming made by the patients. Nicol does not give any further details of Ann's illness, but she obviously recovered. Another nurse, Drusilla Smyth, was not so lucky and died in April. She was buried in the Protestant burial-ground of the town.

Although far from the battlegrounds, the staff at the hospital were, at times, not entirely free from danger. Gangs of Greek brigands roamed the countryside, and on 10th June, Dr. McRaith was captured by them and a ransom of £3,000 demanded. This was later reduced to £400, and after more than a week of chasing the gang through the countryside, the ransom was paid, the money being put up by the local pasha. Dr. McRaith was returned to his family, but it was said that the gang were determined to take any of the hospital staff they could get their hands on, thinking they were worth a high ransom. Dr. McRaith said that the gang would not take women staff, but Dr. Meyer gave orders that nurses were not to go out without a proper escort of medical men and revolvers.

Another horror, which struck in the month of June, was a plague of locusts, which Nicol described as looking like:

"a brown snow-storm ... the ground was completely and thickly covered by them, and they still continued to shower down."

She herself was covered with them, and they got inside her dress, up her sleeves, under her veil and on her neck. The shower continued for about two hours, and they remained in the neighbourhood for about a month. The shore was:

"inches thick with their putrid carcasses, which were so offensive, that one Sunday afternoon the service .... had to be given up."

Fish ate them, which rendered them in turn inedible. The poultry also fed on them, which turned their eggs bright red and made both the birds and their eggs inedible. The locusts were very destructive, eating the shoots on the vines, the orange trees and other crops, even the fabric of clothes and furnishings.

During the summer of 1855, the hospital at Smyrna had emptied out, and there was little hope of more patients being sent. Some of the medical staff had volunteered to be sent elsewhere, and some were talking of returning to England. Lady Nurse Nicol was able to spend two months at the nearby town of Boudjah with the wife of the chaplain and her two children.

Mrs. Coote had resigned as Lady Superintendent on 23rd June, and she and Dr. Coote had gone to the new hospital at Renkioi where Dr. Coote was one of the senior surgeons.

Then, one of the doctors, who had gone to work at the camps, returned through ill health and brought 61 patients with him. This was the beginning of a revival, and *"things were immediately put in working order in hopes of a further reinforcement."*

There were now 6 lady nurses and 17 nurses, one of whom was Ann Hely. The long awaited fall of Sevastopol in September brought a lot more work to the hospital and a contingent of 161 patients.

Lady Nurse Nicol wrote:

"Great was every one's eagerness and alacrity at the news: we all hastened down to the hospital, in the hopes of having our hands full; and I stood in great expectation near the top of the staircase in my division, where Dr. Meyer and other officials received and registered each man as he came in, sending them on to the various divisions afterwards."

On this occasion, she was disappointed, as there were no surgical cases for her division, the vast majority of patients being medical cases. She was not, however, idle for long. There were some bad cases among the newly arrived invalids, and Nicol was one of the "lady nurses" who volunteered to sit up all night with them.

The following day, another transport arrived with 215 patients.

Nicol wrote:

"Now we were indeed all sure of occupation, and great was the bustle we were thrown into..... How pleased we all were to be at work again! All was life and activity with us and we devoted all our energies to the work. My division was principally filled with men who had gunshot wounds, some of them very bad, or had been hurt by shells. One poor fellow had his jaw all shattered, the bone was coming away piece-meal, and his face was swollen to a frightful size. He could not speak, that is to say, not so as to be understood, and we were obliged to guess what he wanted. It was very difficult to feed him, for his appetite was good, and Mr. Holthouse, who was head surgeon of the division, wished him rather to be kept up and well fed; but the trouble was to contrive something which would not stick in the wound inside his mouth, as that always produced great inflammation."

By this time, there were 125 patients in each division. Some of the medical divisions had two "Lady Nurses", but Nicol was the only one in hers. Everyone was very hard worked, but at the same time very pleased to be so.

In such circumstances, the last thing any of them expected was that the hospital would be closed down. It was, therefore, with much *"consternation, astonishment and dismay"* that they received the news on 9th November from Colonel Lefroy that the hospital was, indeed, to be closed and converted into barracks for the Swiss Legion. The patients, and some of the staff, including Ann Hely, were to be sent to Renkioi.

Lady Nurse Nicol returned to England in December 1855.

6 Transfer to Renkioi Hospital

Ann Hely left Smyrna at 3 p.m. on 19th November 1855, on board the ship *Melbourne,* with 115 sick and 23 wounded men on board. They were accompanied by 2 sergeants and 23 orderlies. They arrived at Renkioi at 6 p.m. the following day, but did not disembark until 10 a.m. on 21st November. The operation took two hours[17].

Lady Nurse Nicol visited Renkioi on her way home, and if her reaction is anything to go by, Ann would have been pleasantly surprised by her new place of work. Nicol described it as *"most admirable"* and remarked that it had the advantage over *"poor old Smyrna"* that it was purpose built. She particularly admired the washing and bathing departments, the *"nice fresh"* paint and commented that *"it seemed a very healthy, pleasant place and the air was very fresh and good."*

On arrival, Ann would have been assigned to a ward, where she would have worked under one of the five lady sisters. Dr. Edmund Parkes was the Superintendent in charge of the whole hospital, but he had not worked elsewhere in Turkey, or the Crimea, so would not have been known to Ann. One familiar face would have been Dr. Holmes Coote, who had been appointed Divisional Surgeon along with Dr. Spencer Wells. Ann would have known both of them from Smyrna. They were, however, very senior medical officers, second in rank only to the Superintendent, so Ann would not have had much contact with them on a daily basis.

No direct references to Ann's experiences at Renkioi have come to light, but we do know a great deal about Renkioi Hospital, how it came about, and how it was organized, which does throw some light on what life would have been like for those that worked there.

7 The Building of Renkioi Hospital[18]

During the terrible winter of 1854-55, the need for more, and better, hospital accommodation was realized by the British government, and on 16th February, Sidney Herbert asked Isambard Kingdom Brunel to undertake the design of a new prefabricated hospital. He agreed the same day and worked with great speed, consulting Dr. Edmund Parks, who was to take charge of the new hospital, and other medical personnel as necessary. Brunel quickly acquired a remarkable grasp of the requirements, noting the importance of good water supply, sanitation and ventilation, proper cooking and laundry facilities, warmth and comfort.

The initial plan was for a hospital with 1,000 beds. Dr. Edmund Parkes inspected Brunel's design and found it perfectly satisfactory in every respect. Parkes' task then was to travel to Turkey to choose a suitable site. He arrived on 18th April, and on 3rd May, after various possible sites had been considered, it was eventually decided that a place on the Dardanelles was the best option, despite its rather long distance from the seat of war. It was near the village of Erenkioi, from which the hospital was to take its name. Dr. Parkes later wrote in his report that the site had:

"every requisite, viz., a healthy soil, abundant and good water, a level yet sloping surface, proximity to the sea, good anchorage, and tolerably sheltered landing places."

It was also on a direct line by sea to England, for transport steamers, mail ships, and store ships.

Once the site had been selected, it was decided to increase the capacity of the hospital to 2,000 or 2,500. At this time, it was thought that a smaller hospital, based on the same design, would be erected at Smyrna for 500 patients. This plan never came about, and so the plans for Renkioi were expanded again for it to contain 3,000 beds.

Brunel's plan was for a series of individual wooden buildings, linked by a long wooden corridor with open sides. There was to be a central line of 34 buildings which would contain 1,500 beds; two parallel lines of 17 buildings would contain a further 750 beds each.

Each building was to be 100 ft. long, 40 ft. wide, and 25 ft. high at the apex of the pitched roof. Each one would contain one ward of 50 beds arranged in four rows with a low partition down the middle. A generous 1,200 cubic feet of air was allowed per patient. There was a row of high windows along both lengths of the wards that opened into the fresh air allowing plenty of light and cross ventilation. There were also openings in the gable ends and a fan was installed at one end, capable of forcing 1000 to 1,500 cubic feet of air per minute into pipes under the floor. These pipes had regular vents allowing the air to escape into the ward. The fans had to be manually operated, but fortunately, it was found that they were never needed because of the regular sea breezes.

There was a plentiful supply of fresh clean water piped in from nearby springs, and sewage was flushed by seawater and carried some distance out to sea. The wards were fitted with stoves for heating purposes and lit by candles in specially constructed lamps and lanterns to guard against fire. Each ward had hot water supplied by a small boiler heated with candles, and there were bathrooms fitted with wash basins with running water, flush toilets and urinals. Brunel was most concerned that the flush toilets should be used properly and issued written instructions to ensure that this happened. Canvas baths were supplied, into which even the more disabled patients could be lowered on a frame or sack. Only 30 of the 34 buildings in the central line were wards; the rest were dispensaries and stores. There were also three storehouses near the sea, by one of the jetties, conveniently placed for unloading from ships and connected to the main hospital by horse-drawn railway. Separate kitchen and laundry buildings were built of iron, to help protect against fire.

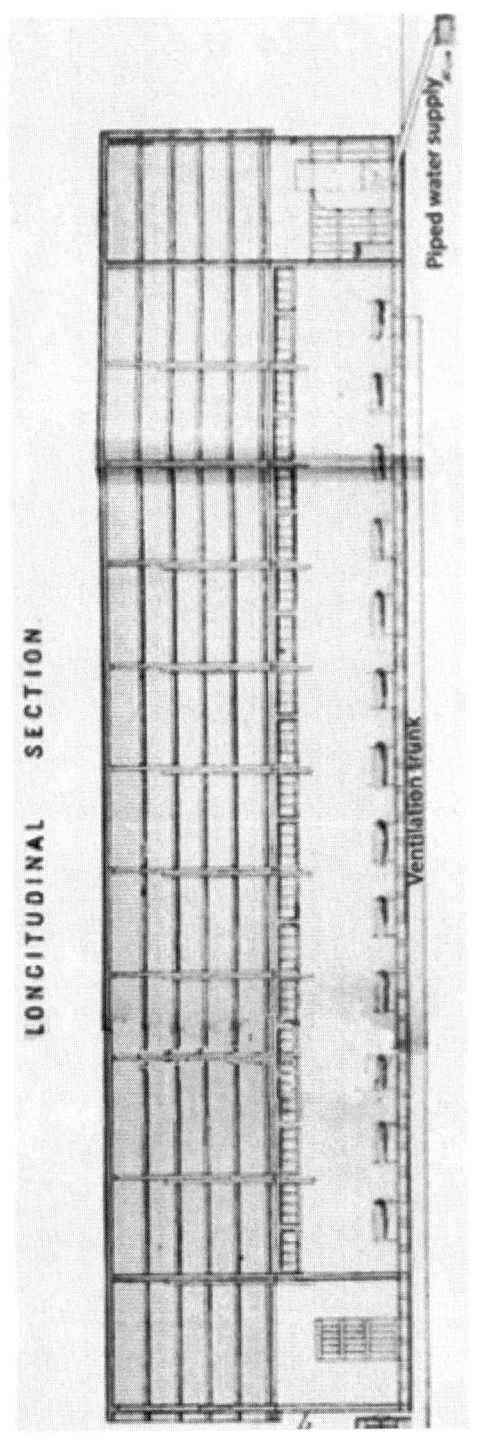

Longitudinal section of a ward at Renkioi hospital. Source: Parkes, E. A. *Report on the Formation and Management of Renkioi Hospital on the Dardanelles, Turkey, 1856.*

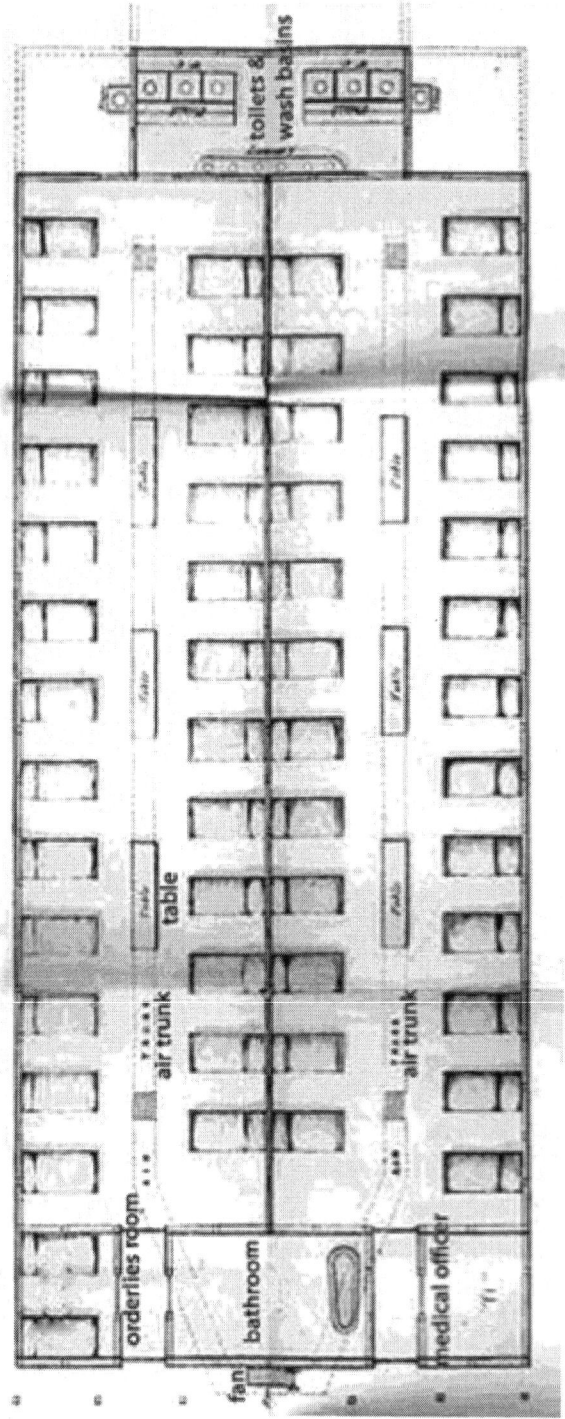

Plan of a ward at Renkioi hospital. Source: Parkes, E. A.

Map showing the layout of the hospital buildings at Renkioi.
Source: Parkes, E. A

Water was carried from springs in earthenware pipes, and then along the length of the wooden corridor by an iron pipe. From that ran lead pipes carrying the water to each ward. This gave a continuous supply of running water without the need for pumps. Sewage was efficiently flushed out to sea. The laundries alone used 4,000 gallons of water a day, and it was thought necessary to supply at least 25,000 gallons a day to the hospital as a whole.

The buildings were manufactured in England and shipped out to Turkey in May 1855. Erection started on 21st May and was carried out under the supervision of the engineer, Mr. Brunton, and his junior Mr. Eassie. Eighteen English workmen were employed, as Brunton did not want to entrust the work to locals. There were 13 carpenters, 1 pipe-layer, 3 plumbers, and a smith. By 12th July, the hospital was ready for 300 patients and by 11th August for 500. Work continued until March 1856, but the hospital was never built to the original planned capacity. By this time, it could contain 2,200 beds, but the number of patients in the hospital at any one time never exceeded 640.

Although the speed with which the hospital buildings were erected was not great, Dr Parkes praised the care with which it was undertaken. The wards were warm, dry and comfortable and never suffered any significant damage even in the worst winter weather.

8 The Staffing and Organisation of Renkioi Hospital

The wards on the central corridor were divided into three divisions of 10 wards each. Each division provided for 500 patients. The two side corridors formed two further divisions, each one providing for 750 patients.

Dr. Parkes, as Superintendent, was in overall charge of the whole hospital. In his report of 1856, he said that each division operated as a separate hospital in its own right. Each division had its own iron kitchen in a separate building. It also had its own dispensary, purveyor's provisions store, utensil store, pack store and matron's linen store.

Each division had either one surgeon or physician assigned to it, who had the overall responsibility for the supervision of medical treatment, cleanliness and hygiene. Each ward of 50 patients had its own medical officer, who was an assistant surgeon or assistant physician, responsible for treatment, cleanliness, hygiene and discipline on the ward. Each division had one "lady sister", 10 nurses and one ward-master in charge of 40 orderlies.

Each ward medical officer reported daily to the divisional officer who in turn reported to the Superintendent. The role of the latter was purely supervisory and administrative. He was not directly concerned with treatment, except in special cases.

A purveyor was in charge of supplies for the whole hospital, and he had a staff of assistants and clerks who saw to the issue of supplies and utensils to each division from the central stores near the jetty. The apothecary, who was also an assistant physician, had a staff of four dispensers, and his store would have been organized on similar lines to that of the purveyor, had the hospital ever reached anything like capacity.

In the laundry, a London laundress organized a team of Greek washerwomen under the supervision of the laundry superintendent. The latter had invented a horse-drawn laundry-van that contained a boiler, washing machine, and drying cabinet. This was designed to be of use at army camps near the fighting, but whether they ever actually existed is not known.

There were two iron laundry buildings at one end of the long central corridor. As well as equipment for washing laundry, they contained drying cabinets, which could be used, not only for drying laundry in wet weather, but also for fumigating items. They could be heated to a temperature of 400° F, which was enough to kill off the vermin with which the men's coats, shirts and blankets were often swarming.

Dirty linen was collected from the wards daily, and the orderly collecting it would itemise it and hand a list to the nurse. She would take this to the divisional linen store from where an equivalent number of items would be issued.

The following account of the staff is given in Dr. Parkes' report of 1856.

Male staff
1 Superintendent
2 Divisional physicians
2 Divisional surgeons
13 Assistant physicians, one of whom was also the apothecary
7 Assistant surgeons
1 Clinical clerk
2 Purveyors
5 Purveyors' clerks
1 Superintendent clerk
1 Store accountant
1 Assistant accountant
4 Dispensers
1 Superintendent of laundry

In addition, there were a number of male orderlies, the engineer and his workmen, together with a number of military men who were attached to the hospital.

There were three "classes" of male orderlies:
1. Civilians, 2. Soldiers sent out from Chatham who were unfit for active service, 3. Soldiers who had been patients in the hospital and had volunteered to stay on temporarily as orderlies. 33 orderlies were entirely engaged in nursing, and 9 others combined this with other duties, e.g. orderly dispenser.[19]

Dr Parkes said of the orderlies:

"In three or four instances men were found, who had a remarkable aptitude for nursing, and took a pleasure in it; they possessed all the feminine sympathy, kindness, and consideration, and were as much liked by the sick men as the nurses. But generally the orderlies, however attentive and kind they might be to the sick, were better adapted for the rough work of the wards."

Female nursing staff[20]
20 Nurses
5 Lady nurses (4 of whom were paid and one, Miss Parkes, was an unpaid volunteer)
The duties of the nurses were confined to actual nursing. All cleaning and "outdoor work" was done by the orderlies, who were male.

The duties of the lady nurses were:
Mrs. Newman,	Superintendent or Matron, with general control over nurses and linen.
Miss Raynes	Sub-matron, occupied full-time assisting Mrs. Newman.
Miss Griesdale	Sub-matron, duties the same as Miss Raynes.
Miss Parkes	superintended the nurses. Spent the whole day on the wards and supervised the distribution of extras and wine.
Miss Frodsham	as for Miss Parkes

The paid nurses are not named in the above report (but see Appendix 1), but they carried out general nursing duties and kept the key to the small supply of extras on each ward. At first, there were two nurses to each ward of 50 men, but this was later reduced to one.

Dr Parkes had this to say of the paid nurses:

"No doubt, for such a duty, the paid nurses must be carefully selected: gathered as our nurses were on the pressure of the moment, there were a few who were not favourable types of their class. But as the inefficient and disorderly nurses were gradually got rid of, and their places supplied by proper persons, the nursing of the soldiers would have been better than in any of the hospitals I am acquainted with in this country, while the only objections that have any weight against the system of female nursing, would have lost all force and application."

Unlike at Smyrna, where we have a first-hand account written by one of the lady nurses, for Renkioi there is no record of the hours worked by the various members of staff. The medical staff visited the wards at 9.30 a.m. and again in the evening. The orderly officer went round the division twice in the night, covering perhaps a quarter of a mile in doing so. There is no indication as to whether or not nurses worked nights, but given that there was at one time only one nurse to a ward, it seems unlikely that nights shifts could have been a regular requirement for nurses.

As well as separate sleeping accommodation, the medical staff (i.e. surgeons and physicians) ate separately from the nurses and had a *"very handsome mess room"* with servants to wait on them.[21] Breakfast was at 7.30 a.m. and the main meal of the day at 2 p.m. Tea or supper with meat and eggs was at 8 p.m. Some of the doctors dressed for their main meal, so it appears to have been a very formal affair. The nurses were further segregated with lady nurses having separate dining facilities to those of the paid nurses.

9 The Work of Renkioi Hospital

From July to October 1855, the only patients in the hospital were local workmen and sailors from passing ships. By the time Ann Hely arrived in November, there had only been one previous transport ship from the war zone carrying 183 sick and 32 wounded soldiers. The total number of patients in the hospital at the time she began work there is not known, but it seems likely to have been in the region of 400.

From October 1855 to February 1856, 11 ships carrying patients arrived from Balaklava and Smyrna. The ships travelled at half speed in order to make the voyage more comfortable for the passengers, and so the journeys took longer than might be expected. Sometimes, the ships called first at Scutari for orders; at other times they came direct to Renkioi. The average sailing time from Balaklava was as follows:

If stopping at Scutari first	86 ¾ hours
Without calling at Scutari	72 ½ hours
Fastest passage (non-stop)	42 hours

Only four deaths occurred amongst the patients whilst in transit and one within twenty-four hours of landing which, Parkes remarked, was a testimony to the good conditions and care on board.

Over the whole time the hospital was open, the total number of admissions of soldiers from the war zone was 1,244. Added to this were a few local workmen and soldiers who had not been on active service, making an overall total of 1,331. Of these, 961 were cured, 320 were invalided home and 50 died.

When Ann Hely was interviewed in 1897, the cases that seemed to have made the biggest impression on her memory were those of gunshot wounds and frostbite. In fact, because of the distance from the fighting, only men with old wounds, sustained in August or September arrived at Renkioi. This is also reflected in the proportion of surgical to medical cases which was said to have been between 25 and 30 per cent.

According to Parkes, the worst cases received were those of frostbite, which often affected both feet, and sometimes the hands as well, so it is not surprising that these remained strongly in Ann's memory. Parkes said that such cases were not as numerous as in the winter of 1854, but were very severe. Often the sufferers were also afflicted with diarrhoea and lung diseases.

Distressing as the frostbite cases were, they were nowhere near as numerous as those suffering from various fevers, dysentery and diarrhoea:

Disease	Admissions	Deaths
Febris continua (fever)	242	13
Dysentery	169	10
Diarrhoea	105	3
Frost-bite	35	2
Gunshot wounds	63	1

During the winter months, fever cases, especially of the type called spotted typhus, were very frequent. It is a flea-borne disease that most commonly occurs in colder months, and in areas where overcrowding and poor hygiene are common, so the war zone camps were excellent breeding grounds for it. It was extremely contagious, and it was felt that a number of men had picked it up while on the transport ships travelling to Renkioi. It was particularly prevalent among the men of the Land Transport Corps, whose general condition with regard to health and cleanliness was said to be even worse than that of common soldiers in the camps. Despite the severity of the disease, deaths from it were relatively low.

The climate around the region where the hospital was situated was conducive to convalescence, and men were encouraged to get out into the fresh air as soon as they were strong enough. The long wooden corridor, being covered, but open-sided, and a third of a

Patients from Renkioi with the hospital seen in the distance. Source: Illustrated News 1st December 1855.

mile long, provided ample opportunity for men to exercise, even in winter. In the warmer months, sea-bathing was encouraged and thought to be very beneficial.

Food supplies were good, with plenty of fruit and vegetables being grown locally. Only milk was in short supply, but in summer and autumn, the supply of goats' milk was said by Parkes to be excellent.

Patients received a good supply of newspapers and books and were also supplied with draughts, chess, backgammon and cribbage boards. Quoits and football were popular outdoor pastimes.

To modern eyes, the ratio of staff, particularly nursing staff, to patients seems to have been alarmingly low. At the time, however, life at Renkioi was believed to be relatively pleasant. Christopher Silver, in his book about Renkioi, states that for much of the life of the hospital, the medical and nursing staff had too little, rather than too much, to do and some had time to pursue outside interests such as photography, meteorology and even ethnology.[22] Dr. Parkes was said to be *"always willing to give short leave for any good purpose to those whose services were not really required."*[23] Some of the doctors went on sightseeing travels. Others volunteered to go and work at the front for a while, especially after the fall of Sevastopol in September 1855. Dr. John Beddoe, in his book *Memories of Eighty Years*, devotes over 60 pages to his time spent at Renkioi, but says almost nothing about the hospital or its work. Most of his writing is devoted to describing his many trips to places of interest in Turkey.

10 Bashi Bazooks

Smyrna was not the only place where nurses and others at the hospital came under threat from local bands. At Renkioi, the threat came not from bandits but from a group of irregular soldiers known as Bashi Bazooks. This group was made up mainly of Turkish soldiers who were notorious for being excellent horsemen, but very undisciplined.

Postcard of a group of Bashi Bazouks. Source: Wikipedia (Creative Commons licence) https://en.wikipedia.org/wiki/Bashi-bazouk accessed 6th October 2016.

They had an encampment ten miles from Renkioi and, according to *The Times* correspondent, were in the habit of:

"riding ventre a terre, and fully armed, through the narrow, and now usually crowded streets of the Dardanelles."

Anyone taking issue with them, or causing anything which they felt to be an insult, would be likely to be stabbed or shot with a pistol.

According to Brunton, the engineer at Renkioi, a column of these men were, on one occasion, seen approaching the hospital in the evening, laden with sheep, fowls, geese, grain, and other commodities stolen from nearby farms where the farmers had been murdered.[24]

The Times correspondent wrote that the event took place in July 1855, before Ann Hely arrived at Renkioi, and that it was 130 Bashi Bazook deserters who shouted *"No buono Inglesi"* as they approached.

At the news of their coming, Brunton had informed the British and Turkish authorities and arranged for the arming of the men in the hospital compound, while women and children were taken off to anchored ships for safety. Brunton's men fired on the approaching column, causing the Bashi Bazooks to retreat. According to Brunton, one later became a patient in the hospital.

On another occasion, *The Times* correspondent himself was confronted, when one of the Bashi Bazooks "in his cups" pushed open his unlocked door in the middle of the night and held a gun to his head. The arrival of the correspondent's friend persuaded the man to withdraw, and after that, sentries were placed beyond the lines of the buildings. This apparently reassured the ladies of their safety to the extent that they could *"ride about freely and as late as in any English county."* How true this was, and how much the Bashi Bazooks would have impinged on Ann Hely's experience in Renkioi, is impossible to say, but she was most likely to have been aware of their presence.

However, for many of the junior medical staff, and this really refers to the junior doctors rather than the nurses, life could be generally rather pleasant and leisurely. According to Holmes Coote, the senior medical officer who had accompanied Ann Hely on her journey out to Smyrna, at Renkioi, the staff:

"being isolated from the outer world, could turn their attention to elegant pursuits. Life in [Renkioi] was a perfect calm. A wandering Bashi bazooka, a shower of rain or a flight of wild ducks threw a whole encampment into a flutter of surprise. The life was pleasant but with something of a tameness in it."[25]

11 Later Life

By the beginning of 1856, the war had reached its final stages, and the number of sick and wounded was much reduced. The last shipload of patients arrived at Renkioi on 8th February 1856, and after that there were very few admissions. Peace was declared in March of that year, and by July, all military hospitals were closed. The last patients were discharged from Renkioi in June 1856, and all the staff had left by the end of July.

Very little is known of Ann's life between her return to England in the summer of 1856, and the time she became a resident of the Ravenstone Hospital almshouses. When she was interviewed by the press in 1897, she said that on her return she had:

"held positions of trust in the house-holds of various noblemen, her last post being that of housekeeper to the Marquis of Zetland."[26]

She stated that she had been selected to nurse the mother of Queen Victoria, the Duchess of Kent, but that Her Royal Highness had died at about the time Mrs. Hely was to have taken up the position.[27] She also claimed to have nursed Florence Nightingale herself. There is no evidence to support this, but a rather enigmatically worded set of notes in the archives at Ravenstone, apparently written by Nightingale, seem to indicate that she did know Ann Hely:

"I do not remember that Dr. P. had a Hospital on the "Dardanelles" – But as I said, information as to what he did was not official but only friendly.

"I remember the name Renkioi.

"Mrs. Hely was a perfectly respectable woman; the widow of a village apothecary.

"She was recommended to me by Dr. Parkes, <u>not</u> on my return from the Crimean War. [I did without any maid of my own for some years, I think] but afterwards. She had no capacity for either maid or nurse, but <u>then</u> no <u>nurse</u> was a <u>nurse</u> and she was <u>quite</u> respectable."

No trace has been found to date of Ann Hely in any Census records for 1861, 1871 or 1881. The minutes of the Trustees of Ravenstone Hospital show that she was offered one of the almshouses in October 1889, and the Census for Ravenstone shows her to be resident there in 1891 and 1901.

In 1897, she was awarded the order of the Royal Red Cross for her nursing service in the Crimea. The order had been founded in 1883 by Queen Victoria to recognize the work of nurses who had been recommended for special devotion or competency while engaged on nursing or hospital duties with British military forces. Florence Nightingale was the first to receive the award, and according to the *Leicester Chronicle* report at the time, only 76 women had been awarded the honour, prior to Ann Hely. Among them were said to be the Empress Frederick of Germany, the (then) Princess of Wales, and six other Princesses.

Ann Hely was invited to attend an award ceremony at Windsor Castle, but was considered too frail to travel such a distance. Special permission was therefore granted for the investiture to happen in Ravenstone.

The ceremony took place in a room belonging to the Rector, the Reverend Vandeleur, who also presided over the proceedings, supported by the Master of the Hospital, the Reverend Dr. Barber. The Order was presented to Ann Hely by Lady Cave Browne Cave of Rotherwood House, Ashby de la Zouch. Various dignitaries were present (a full list is given in the *Leicester Chronicle* report which is reproduced in full at Appendix 2) as well as other residents of the almshouses.

Both Reverend Vandeleur and Dr. Barber made speeches, Reverend Vandeleur commenting that:

"no work was more noble than the relief of the suffering in such a war, which was a matter now of history…..The honour was not only great to Mrs. Hely, but also to the village of Ravenstone, and fitting in this jubilee year."

Lady Cave then pinned the Order to Mrs. Hely's dress, stating that it was her great pleasure and honour to do so. The assembled company then sang the first verse of the National Anthem, after which, Ann Hely kissed the hand of Lady Cave. Reverend Arthur S. Mammatt, Vicar of Packington, called for cheers for Mrs. Hely *"which were heartily given."*

Reverend Mammatt proposed a vote of thanks to Lady Cave, which was seconded by a Mr. Robert Creswell, who also said a few words. He stated that Mrs. Hely was *"one of his oldest and best friends."* When he was a boy, Mrs. Hely had returned to Ravenstone from the Crimea and nursed him through an illness. He praised her nursing skill saying that:

"though there were scientific nurses of the present day, none could have nursed him with greater kindness and ability."

Creswell's remarks are interesting in that they shed a small light on what happened to Ann Hely after she left Renkioi. It appears that she did return to her home village of Ravenstone in the late 1850s, although by the time of the 1861 Census she was no longer living there. The Creswells were a farming family who lived in *The White House* in the village. Robert Creswell was 11 in the 1861 Census. A member of the Bradshaw family, possibly Ann's neice, was a 14-year-old servant in their house. Ann's brother, Thomas Ayre Bradshaw, was the publican of *The Plough* by this time, as well as continuing with his trade as a blacksmith.

Returning to the proceedings at Ann's investiture, various votes of thanks followed that to Lady Cave. Ann's many lady friends showed great interest in her new Order, which consisted of a Maltese cross, inscribed with the words *Faith, Hope* and *Charity* on three arms and *1883* on the lower arm. In the centre, was a gold medallion inscribed with an image of Queen Victoria, and the cross was attached to a red and blue bow. After the formal proceedings, Lady Cave and her two daughters entertained all the residents of the almshouses to tea in the Rector's room. It was said that they personally assisted with the arrangements, alongside Dr. Barber, his wife and daughter, and others.

Ann Hely died at Ravenstone Hospital on Thursday 5th June 1902.

Appendix 1

Staff list for Renkioi Hospital

Male staff

	Title and First Name	Surname	Employment
1	Dr E A	Parkes	Superintendent
2	Mr Holmes	Coote	Surgeon
3	Mr	Spencer Wells	Surgeon
4	Dr H	Goodeve	Physician
5	Dr W	Robertson	Physician
6	Dr Thomas	Armitage	Assistant Surgeon
7	Dr Charles	Baden	Assistant Surgeon
8	Dr John	Beddoe	Assistant Surgeon
9	Dr	Buchannan	Assistant Surgeon
10	Dr David	Christison	Assistant Surgeon
11	Dr	Cowan	Assistant Surgeon
12	Dr John	Dix	Assistant Surgeon
13	Dr Thomas	Dixon	Assistant Surgeon
14	Dr J?	Fawcas	Assistant Surgeon
15	Dr John	Fox	Assistant Surgeon
16	Dr Thomas	Hale	Assistant Surgeon
17	Dr Thomas	Holland	Assistant Surgeon
18	Dr John	Kirk	Assistant Surgeon
19	Mr	Maunder	Assistant Surgeon
20	Dr James	McClaren	Assistant Surgeon
21	Dr	Perry	Assistant Surgeon
22	Dr Alfred	Playne	Assistant Surgeon
23	Dr William	Reid	Assistant Surgeon
24	Dr	Roberts	Assistant Surgeon
25	Dr Geo	Scott	Assistant Surgeon
26	Mr Samuel	Stretton	Assistant Surgeon
27	Dr Thomas	Veal	Assistant Surgeon
28	Mr J	Humphrey	Apothecary
29	Mr	Baker	Dispenser
30	Mr W H	Clarke	Dispenser
31	Mr William	Roope	Dispenser
32	Mr W	Shepherd	Dispenser
33	Mr William	Wrenn	Hospital Steward
34	Mr H	Greenling	Secretary to Superintendent
35	Mr G	Webster	Store Accountant
36	Mr John M	Pagan	Clinical Clerk
37	John	Smith	Head Baker
38	Alfred	Easy	Assistant Baker
39	Thomas	Adams	Assistant Baker
40	David	Johnson	Assistant Baker

41	Alexdr	Mesvil?	Head Cook
42	James	Jones	Cook
43	C	Mera?	Assistant Cook
44	J	Vannini	Assistant Cook
45	Mr Basil	Hall	Asst. Store Accountant
46	Claris	Crump	Issuer & Cutler
47	Mr J	Hooper	Laundryman
48	Robert	Smith	Orderly, Issuer & Asst. Steward
49	William	Samuel	Orderly - Dispenser
50	B	Clothier	Orderly & Asst. Steward
51	Joseph	Graystone	Orderly & Issuer
52	Charles	Parker	Orderly & Laundry Asst.
53	J	Dickens	Orderly & Store Keeper
54	J	Castle	Orderly & Ward Master
55	Alexander	McDonald	Orderly & Ward Master
56	John	Cross	Orderly to act as Cutler
57	G	Ainslie	Orderly
58	James	Anderson	Orderly
59	Peter	Bathgate	Orderly
60	John	Bricknell	Orderly
61	James	Burnett	Orderly
62	Michael	Callaghan	Orderly
63	D	Clarke	Orderly
64	Geo	Davey	Orderly
65	Frank	Day	Orderly
66	John	Easy	Orderly
67	James	Fitzgerald	Orderly
68	Geo	Forbes	Orderly
69	S	Gilbey	Orderly
70	Alexander	Gordon	Orderly
71	Denis	Hallinan	Orderly
72	T	Humphreys	Orderly
73	W	Hutchinson	Orderly
74	John R	Kyle	Orderly
75	Geo	Leech (Snr)	Orderly
76	Geo	Leech (Jnr)	Orderly
77	John	Manson	Orderly
78	A?	McClelland	Orderly
79	Thomas	McCrearie?	Orderly
80	Robert	McKenzie	Orderly
81	Charles	Miller	Orderly
82	J	Mitchell	Orderly
83	J	Phillips	Orderly
84	Thomas	Poore	Orderly
85	A	Pringle	Orderly
86	Charles	Robertson	Orderly
87	John	Simpson	Orderly
88	J	Somerville	Orderly
89	John	Stark	Orderly
90	William	Watson	Orderly
91	William	Wood	Orderly

92	William	Hicks	Army Works Corps
93	Luke	Shute	Army Works Corps
94	Charles	Vickermann	Artisan

Female Staff

	Title and First name	**Family name**	**employment**
1	Mrs Henrietta E	Newman	Lady Superintendent
2	Miss	Raynes	Sub Matron
3	Miss Elizabeth	Griesdale	Lady Storekeeper
4	Miss	Parkes	Lady Sister
5	Miss Eliza	Frodsham	Lady Nurse
6	Miss Harriet	Hughes	Head Nurse
7	Mrs Elizabeth	Clarke	Upper Nurse
8	Mrs Sarah	James	Upper Nurse
9	Anne	Newman	Upper Nurse
10	Mrs Margaret A	Reid	Upper Nurse
11	Mrs Mary	Viney	Upper Nurse
12	Mrs M	Heley	Nurse
13	Elizabeth	Paxton	Nurse
14	Mrs Ann	Rogers	Nurse
15	Fanny	Warcus/Warens?	Nurse
16	Annie	Blackhall	Nurse & Sempstress
17	Mary Ann	Adams	Nurse & Servant to Lady Superintendent
18	Elizabeth	Amiel	Nurse & Under Laundress
19	Mrs Caroline	Browne	Under Nurse
20	Janet	Duncan	Under Nurse
21	Mrs Margaret	Emslie	Under Nurse
22	Mrs Margaret	Godfrey	Under Nurse
23	Mrs Mary	Grey	Under Nurse
24	Sarah	Grove	Under Nurse
25	Mrs Margaret	Hallinan	Under Nurse
26	Marion	Hepburn	Under Nurse
27	Agnes	Miller	Under Nurse
28	Mrs Isabella	Storer	Under Nurse
29	Mrs Margaret	Wilson	Under Nurse
30	Mrs Rachel	Johnston	Upper Laundress

Source: TNA WO 43/991 The above is a transcript of the original handwritten document made by the website Dorsetbay:
http://www.dorsetbay.plus.com/hist/crimea/chstaff.htm accessed on 7th October 2016.

N.B. Ann Ayre Hely is recorded as M Hely in the list above.
As the original was handwritten, it is easy to see how the
double A (i.e. A A Hely) could have been mistakenly transcribed
as the letter M.

Appendix 2 Transcript of an article in the *Leicester Mercury,* Saturday 18th December 1897.

A CRIMEAN NURSE AT RAVENSTONE.
PRESENTATION OF THE ROYAL RED CROSS.

There was a large assemblage in the Rector's room, Ravenstone, on Wednesday afternoon on the occasion of the presentation of the Royal Red Cross to Mrs. Ann Eyre Hely, an inmate of Ravenstone Hospital, Ashby-de-la-Zouch, who had recently been awarded the coveted honour by her Majesty the Queen. Mrs. Hely is the widow of a surgeon formerly practising at Ravenstone.

In the year 1854, she left England with Dr. Holmes Coote and Mrs. Coote to join Miss Florence Nightingale's staff of nurses in the Crimea. She served under Dr. Parkes at Ranki, *(sic)* in the Dardanelles, from August until after the end of the war, when all the soldiers were convalescent and ready to come home. She had as many as 150 patients under her charge at a time, mostly suffering from frostbites *(sic)* and gunshot wounds.

After her return to England, she nursed Miss Florence Nightingale for some months and subsequently held positions of trust in the households of various noblemen, her last post being that of housekeeper to the Marquis of Zetland. Mrs. Hely is one of the occupiers of 36 almshouses, founded in 1710 by Rebecca Wilkins, and is 78 years of age. To this may be added that she was selected to nurse H.R.H. the late Duchess of Kent, mother of her Majesty the Queen, but H.R.H. died about the time Mrs. Hely was to have commenced her duties.

The state of Mrs. Hely's health prevented her from undertaking the fatigue of a journey to Windsor and the excitement of the presentation of the Order by her Majesty in person. The Rev. Dr. Barber, Master of the Hospital, made the application to the authorities and supplied the necessary particulars on behalf of Mrs. Hely, with the above favourable result. Lady Cave Browne Cave, of

Rotherwood House, Ashby-de-la- Zouch, kindly consented to make the presentation on behalf of the Queen.

Her Ladyship's entry with her daughters into the crowded room was the occasion for applause. There were, together with the heroine of the occasion, the Rev. Dr. Barber, Master of Ravenstone Hospital, Mrs. and Miss Barber, the Rev. G. O. Vandeleur, Mrs. and Miss Vandeleur, Mrs. And Miss Fosbrooke, Miss Freckleton (Ravenstone), Dr. and Mrs. Stabes (Ashby), Mrs. W. E. Smith, the Rev. A. S. Mammatt, Mrs. Mammatt, Mr. and Mrs. and Miss Edge, the Misses Buck (Altons), Dr. Jamie and Mrs. Jamie (Coalville), Dr. and Mrs. Thomas (Ibstock), Mrs. Thos. Jesson (Ashby), Mrs. St. John Ashby, Mr. R. J. and Mrs. Creswell, Mr. G. H. Wooley, Mrs. B. N. Everard (Bardon Lodge), Mrs. J. J. Sharp (Coalville), Mr. H. Vandeleur, and many others, including the inmates of the hospital.

The Rector presided, supported by Dr. Barber, Lady Cave, and the Misses Cave, whilst Mrs. Hely was accorded a prominent position close to Lady Cave. The honoured lady appeared in the best of spirits. She is of tall stature, and, considering her advanced years and experiences in early life, bore up bravely.

The Chairman, rising to open the proceedings, said that the object was explained in the pamphlet written by Dr. Barber. They all knew of the Crimean war, and the terrible sufferings of the troops in the cold winter. It was not till Miss Nightingale formed her band of workers that the sufferings of the troops were in part alleviated. Mrs. Hely was one of the first to go out to carry out the work of nursing, and no work was more noble than the relief of the suffering in such a war, which was a matter now of history. The order was not established until 1883, and one of the first to receive the honour was Miss Nightingale, Mrs. Hely's old friend. (Applause.) The honour was not only great to Mrs. Hely, but also to the village of Ravenstone, and fitting in this jubilee year. (Applause.) The first intention was to have had the order bestowed in person by the Queen, and though Dr. Barber, the Master of the hospital, would have escorted Mrs. Hely safely to the Queen's presence, Mrs. Hely felt that the journey would have been too much for her. In conclusion, he referred to Lady Cave's kindness in attending to present the order, and asked Her Ladyship to present it in the name of the Queen. (Loud applause.)

Dr. Barber referred to several letters he had received from residents of the district, who were invited and unable to attend owing to previous engagements. All expressed regret. Canon Denton had written a kind letter in reference to Mrs. Hely, and those associated with her in her work. Some explanations were due for his reasons in calling the meeting. The order was founded in 1883 from zeal and devotion in providing for and nursing sick and wounded soldiers or sailors in the field, in hospitals, or on board ship. In the 14 years the order had been founded, there had been only 76 who received it, and it could be understood that it was not thoughtlessly or recklessly bestowed. Among the holders were the Queen, the Empress Frederick of Germany, the Princess of Wales, and six other princesses, and Miss Nightingale. (Applause). Mrs. Hely, had she been able, would have had the investiture last Thursday, but having pointed out in a letter to the War Office, that she was indisposed, received a reply to the effect that her Majesty approved of the Royal Red Cross being presented to Mrs. Hely in such a manner as he, Dr. Barber, considered best, and the War Office further requested a statement as to the presentation and the date. He (Dr. Barber) would be happy to forward what was asked for. If Mrs. Hely's health had permitted, the presentation would have been made under more dazzling circumstances. He had invited her friends and the trustees of the Hospital, and the Rector was the first to entertain his (Dr. Barber's) views, and readily lent the room, and they had Lady Cave's kindly assistance and consent to present the order. They formed a happy party, and in having Mrs. Hely as one of their number, they had one esteemed by all. (Applause.) Her name was already published as being one of the recipients of the Order, which was considered of great value by all who possessed it. (Loud applause.)

Lady Cave, having pinned the order to Mrs. Hely's dress, said it afforded her pleasure to perform the duty. The order was a recognition of Mrs. Hely's services in nursing the sick, and she had the great honour of investing Mrs. Hely with the cross in the name of her Majesty the Queen and Empress. (Applause.) During the ceremony the first verse of the National Anthem was sung, and at the conclusion, Mrs. Hely gracefully kissed the hand of Lady Cave and resumed her seat amidst applause.

The Rev. A. S. Mammatt (vicar of Packington) called for cheers for Mrs. Hely, which were heartily given. Rev. A. S. Mammatt moved a vote of thanks to Lady Cave for the graceful way she performed the duty in the name of her Majesty. — Mr. R. G. Creswell seconded the resolution. Referring to Mrs. Hely, he said that she was one of his oldest and best friends, and he was pleased with the honour conferred on her and Ravenstone. (Applause.) When he (Mr. Creswell) was a boy, Mrs. Hely returned to Ravenstone from the Crimea, and, during an illness, he was attended by her, and though there were scientific nurses of the present day, none could have nursed him with greater kindness and ability. (Applause) The vote was carried with acclamation, and Lady Cave briefly returned thanks. Rev. A. S. Mammatt proposed a vote of thanks to Dr. Barber, which Mr. Creswell seconded. — Dr. Barber, replying, said that when he saw that three nurses who were at the Crimea were invested with the order at Windsor, after the jubilee festivities, it occurred to him that Mrs. Hely had been forgotten. He communicated with the War Office, and one day was surprised to see that she had been gazetted with Miss Terrot, daughter of the late Bishop of Edinburgh. The delay in the presentation was due to the fact that Mrs. Hely's health would not permit her to travel to Windsor Castle. He would be able to forward the intimation that the inhabitants were proud of the honour conferred on Mrs. Hely. (Loud applause.)

The order is in the form of a Maltese cross, of rich design, with "Faith," "Hope," and "Charity" on three arms of the cross, and "1883" on the lower arm. There is also a gold medallion of the Queen in the centre. The cross was attached to a red and blue bow, and was the object of considerable interest to the recipient's many lady friends. After the proceedings, Lady Cave and the Misses Cave entertained the whole of the residents of the hospital to tea in the rector's room, and personally assisted in the arrangements with Dr. Barber (the Master) and Mrs. and Miss Barber, and others.

References

Chapter 1 Early Life
[1] Screaton, Colin, *Ann Ayre Hely, a Crimean Nurse,* unpublished essay.
[2] Census of England and Wales 1851, HO107/2084, Folio 679, page 15.
[3] *Ibid.* Folio 678, page 12.
[4] Census of England and Wales 1841, HO 107/675/6 Folio 12, page 18.
[5] Letter from Dr Hely to the Trustees, reproduced in *A History of Ravenstone Hospital,* by Mary Danaher, page 56.
[6] *Leicester Chronicle,* Saturday 12th August 1854 and *Leicester Journal,* Friday 11th August 1854.

Chapter 2 The Crimean War and the Care of the Sick and Wounded
[7] *The Times, 15th* and 22nd September 1854.
[8] Sydney Herbert's letter was published in full in several newspapers at the end of October, including the *London Daily News,* 28th October 1854.
[9] Most sources say that there were 38 nurses. The figure of 40 is taken from a report in the *Taunton Courier and Western Advertiser,* 1st November 1854.
[10] *Medical Times and Gazette,* (1855) 1:138-139, quoted in Shepherd, John *The Crimean Doctors, A History of the British Medical Services in the Crimean War,* Liverpool University Press, 1991, Volume II, page 414.

Chapter 3 The Setting up of Smyrna Hospital
[11] *Op. cit.* Shepherd, John, page 424.
[12] *Ibid,* page 432, quoting from *Medical Times and Gazette,* 1855, 1,347.

Chapter 4 Ann Hely Answers the Call
[13] For example: Silver, Christopher, *Renkioi, Brunel's Forgotten Crimean War Hospital,* Valonia Press, 2007 and *Ismeer or Smyrna and its British Hospital in 1855 by A Lady,* anonymous memoirs of a "lady nurse" (said to be Martha C Nicol) in Smyrna, James Madden, 1856, digitized by the Internet Archive in 2010 and available for download, free of charge from https://archive.org/details/ismeerorsmyrnait00nico
(accessed 3rd September 2016.)
[14] *Ibid.*
[15] *Op. cit.* Shepherd, Vol. II, page 431.

Chapter 5 Nursing in Smyrna Hospital
[16] *Op..cit.* Shepherd, John. P.427.

Chapter 6 Transfer to Renkioi Hospital
[17] *Op.cit.* Silver, Christopher, p. 108, and register of nurses sent out to the East, Florence Nightingale Museum, London.

Chapter 7 The Building of Renkioi Hospital
[18] All the information in this chapter is taken from Parkes, E. D. *Report on the Formation and General Management of Renkioi Hospital on the Dardanelles, Turkey,* 1856, digitised by the Wellcome Library and made available under a Creative Commons Public Domain licence.

Chapter 8 The Staffing and Organisation of Renkioi Hospital
[19] *Op cit.* Silver, Christopher, p. 200.
[20] Slightly different information is given in TNA WO 43/991 which states that there were 28 nurses: 1 Lady Superintendent, Sub Matron, Head Nurse, Lady Nurse, 8 Upper Nurses, 4 Nurses, 11 Under Nurses, 1 Nurse servant, 1 Nurse and Seamstress.
[21] *Op. cit.* Silver, Christopher, p. 131.

Chapter 9 The Work of Renkioi Hospital
[22] *Op. cit.* Silver, Christopher, pp. 133-4.
[23] Beddoe, John, *Memories of Eighty Years,* 1910, p.80.

Chapter 10 Bashi Bazooks
[24] *Op, cit,* Silver, Christopher, pp. 143-144.
[25] Coote, H. *Hospitalism. British Medical Journal;* 1869. I. 565-566, quoted in *op. cit.* Silver, Christopher, pp. 147.

Chapter 11 Later Life
[26] *Leicester Chronicle,* Saturday 18th December, 1897.
[27] The Duchess died on 16 March 1861, at the age of 74.

Short Bibliography

Shepherd, John *The Crimean Doctors, A History of the British Medical Services in the Crimean War,* Liverpool University Press, 1991, Volume II.

Silver, Christopher, *Renkioi, Brunel's Forgotten Crimean War Hospital,* Valonia Press, 2007.

Ismeer or Smyrna and its British Hospital in 1855 by A Lady, anonymous memoirs of a "lady nurse" (said to be Martha C Nicol) in Smyrna, James Madden, 1856, digitized by the Internet Archive in 2010 and available for download, free of charge from https://archive.org/details/ismeerorsmyrnait00nico (accessed 3rd September 2016.

Danaher, Mary, *A History of Ravenstone Hospital,* 2016.

Parkes, E. D. *Report on the Formation and General Management of Renkioi Hospital on the Dardanelles, Turkey,* 1856, digitised by the Wellcome Library and made available under a Creative Commons Public Domain licence.

Index

A

Admissions · 15, 35-36, 42

B

Balaklava · 4, 35
Barber, Dr · 43-45, 50-54
Bashi Bazooks · 39-41
baths · 24, 26
Bradshaw · 1, 44
brigands · 21
Brunel, Isambard Kingdom · 25-30
Brunton, engineer · 30, 40

C

Cave Brown Cave, Lady · 43-45, 50-54
Charge of the Light Brigade · 4, 5
closure of Smyrna · 23
Coote, Holmes · 8, 11, 13, 22, 24, 40, 46, 50
Creswell, Robert · 44, 51-53

D

death of John Hely · 2
Deaths · 15, 35, 36

E

Eassie, assistant engineer · 30

F

Forrester, Lady Maria · 5
Fosbrooke · 1, 51

H

Hely, Dr John Joseph · 1-3
Herbert, Sydney · 5, 25

L

lady nurses · 9, 11, 13, 16-23
laundry · 26, 32, 33

M

Mammatt, Arthur Simmonds · 44, 51, 53
Marriage of Ann Bradshaw/Hely · 2
Messagerie Imperiale · 12
Meyer, Dr John · 9, 16, 19, 21, 22

N

Nicol, Martha C · 11, 13-23
Nightingale, Florence · 5, 6, 10, 42, 43, 50, 51, 52
nuns · 9

P

Parkes, Dr Edmund · 24, 25, 30, 31-34, 35-38, 43
plague of locusts · 11-12
Plough Inn · 1, 2, 44

R

ransom · 21
register of nurses · 10, 11, 19
Regulation dress · 19-20
Renkioi – 10, 24-41, 46-49
Royal Red Cross · 11, 50, 57, 59
Russell, William · 5

S

Scutari · 5-6, 8, 35,
Sevastopol · 22, 38
sewage, Renkioi · 26, 29
Sinai · 12, 13
Smyrna · 8-9, 11, 13-23, 25
Smyth, Drusilla · 21
Spencer Wells, Thomas · 8 - 9, 11, 27, 53

T

toilets · 26

V

Vandeleur, Reverend · 55, 43-44
ventilation · 25, 26

W

water supply, Renkioi · 25-26, 29
Webb, Reverend · 2

Z

Zetland, Marquis · 42, 50

#0143 - 221216 - C0 - 229/152/4 - PB - DID1699705